Learning to be a Durable Person

Social and Emotional Skill Building Activities
for
K – 5 Gifted and Talented Children
by
Dr. Mary Hennenfent, Ed.D.

ISBN 978-1-59363-239-7

© 2008 Prufrock Press Inc.

Preface

What is a durable person? A durable person is a person who can survive the day-to-day struggles of life and still be satisfied, productive, and happy. Why do we want this for gifted children? I believe as educators we want this for all children. However, gifted children present a uniqueness when addressing their social and emotional needs. For a gifted child to meet both academic and social potentials, care and support must be provided for their emotional needs. There are many manuals on surviving giftedness. I want students to thrive, not just survive.

This curriculum is designed to allow a gifted child to explore their own giftedness, expand social skills, cultivate leadership skills, and develop strategies for combating stress, anger and perfectionism. Gifted children need to be taught to be durable, so they can continue to be responsible and productive citizens.

We would like to credit Dr. Howard Gardner for his Multiple Intelligence categories and descriptions. It is wonderful that we have a place to start to understand and identify strengths in ourselves and others.

Dr. J.P. Guilford and Dr. E. Paul Torrance first identified the FFOE approach to divergent thinking. This acronym for Fluency, Flexibility, Originality, and Elaboration is widely used by classroom teachers of the gifted.

Acknowledgements

A special thank you to Brenda McGee and Debbie Keiser for taking a risk and believing in me.

A special thank you to Tom LaRosa for pushing me to strive for my dreams, to Judy Bliggenstorfer for inspiring me as a gifted educator, and to Pat Curry and Jennifer Burke for your positive encouragement throughout this process.

A special thank you to my family for supporting me with quiet, uninterrupted writing time.

Written by: Dr. Mary Hennenfent, Ed. D.
Cover Design by: Brandon Bolt
Edited by: Debbie Keiser, Brenda McGee, and Linda Triska

NOTE

The Web sites in this curriculum were working and age-appropriate at the time of publication, but Prufrock Press has no control over any subsequent changes.

Table of Contents

Essential Understandings and Guiding Questions

Being gifted means different things to different people.
- What does it mean to be gifted?
- How are gifted students perceived by friends, teachers, and parents?
- What is the difference between self-esteem and self image?
- Who are you as a person?
- How can we celebrate personal differences?

A person who chooses a career based on his or her intelligences may be more productive and satisfied in his or her career.
- What multiple intelligences do you have?
- Which career best suits your intelligences?
- Should your career choice be based on its ability to support the lifestyle of your choice?
- Should you choose a career based on passion or on potential earnings?

Successful people exhibit the traits of creativity, goal setting, intelligence, courage and kindness.
- Why is goal setting important?
- How are you motivated? Intrinsically or extrinsically?
- How are you creative?
- How can gifted students exhibit courage?
- How can gifted students show regard for others on a daily basis?
- Should gifted students go to a specialized school?
- How do creativity and different thinking make learning more enjoyable?
- How can gifted children show responsibility and respect for others?
- How do peoples' differences make the world a richer place to live?
- How can we treat people with disabilities with respect?

Understanding why people tease others may allow you to choose how to deal with teasing.
- Why do people tease each other?
- What should you do when you are teased?

6

Stress is in our everyday lives. Learning to recognize personal stressors may allow you to diffuse stress appropriately.

- What types of things cause you stress?
- How does your body react to stress?
- How can you reduce stress?
- How can I make my problems solvable?

We experience a range of emotions everyday. Anger is a normal emotion, how you deal with your anger is a choice.

- What emotions do you experience in everyday situations?
- What things make you angry?
- How can you handle the emotion of anger?
- What are my various emotions?

Making and keeping friends may help alleviate stress.

- How do you make a friend?
- How do you keep a friend?
- What do you do when you have a problem with a friend?
- What qualities do you look for in a friend?
- What qualities do you possess as a potential friend?
- Should you have a lot of friends or just a few friends?

No one is perfect.

- What is perfectionism?
- How do others influence your desire to be perfect?
- Should a person try to be perfect?
- How can you be more honest?

Notes

_____

_____

_____

_____

_____

_____

_____

_____

_____

_____

_____

_____

_____

_____

_____

_____

_____

_____

_____

_____

_____

_____

_____

_____

_____

_____

UNIT 1

Being gifted means different things to different people.

9

Activity 1 – I'm in the Bag

Grades: K - 5

Instructional Materials
- brown paper bag tied with ribbon (1 per student)
- magazines
- note cards
- scissors
- resealable sandwich bags
- copies of Attachment 1

Enduring Understanding
Being gifted means different things to different people.

Guiding Question
What does it mean to be gifted?

Preparation
Prepare a brown paper lunch bag ahead of time by folding over the top of the bag, punch two holes in the flap and thread a ribbon through the holes.

Introduction
Give each student a pencil and a piece of paper. Challenge students to answer the question, "What does it mean to be gifted?" Have students share their answers. Record the traits they mention on the board. Create a chart of the traits students mention.

A. Give each student a brown paper lunch bag tied with a ribbon. Ask students to put their names on the outside of the bag.

B. Invite students to think about things they like and activities at which they excel.

C. Distribute note cards, magazines and scissors. Have students cut out pictures or draw things they like and activities at which they excel.

D. Invite students to share their examples. Place a tally mark next to the traits on the board if they are shared. Have students place all examples in a resealable sandwich bag.

E. Tell students this time they will be putting examples of things they dislike or things that they are not good at in the bag. Have students repeat Step C.

F. Have students share their examples. Ask students why they think these traits were not listed on the board. Explain that being a person who is gifted is more than just having positive traits. Gifted people have strengths and weaknesses as well. Ask students if other students in their class would be considered gifted based on their list.

Assessment

A. Have students separate the traits into two categories: traits exhibited by gifted people and traits exhibited by high achievers. Challenge students to create a graphic organizer to display this information. Based on the grade level or your students, encourage them to rewrite their definitions of giftedness using the graphic organizer.

B. Score students based on the rubric on Attachment 1.

> **Teacher Tip**
> Keeping the bags each year and revisiting the definitions of giftedness will show student growth.

Notes

_____

_____

_____

_____

_____

_____

_____

_____

_____

_____

_____

_____

_____

_____

_____

_____

_____

_____

_____

Name_____ Score _____/18

Content Standard	Standard	Student Assessment	Facilitator Assessment
Topic is listed as the title.	3		
There are 2 subtopics labeled gifted people only and high achievers only	3		
A new definition for giftedness is written utilizing the subtopic for gifted people only.	3		
Skill Standard			
Graphic organizer is arranged in a clear logical manner.	3		
All spelling is accurate.	3		
Items under subtopics are classified correctly.	3		

4= Exceeds standard
3= Meets standard
2= Nearing standard
1= below standard

Activity 2 - Better At or Better Than

Grades: K - 3

Instructional Materials
- copies of Attachment 2

Introduction

Have students determine the difference between the following statements:
"I am better at math than others."
"I am better than others at math."
Discuss the subtle difference. Explain that the perception other people have of them is based on how they act.

Enduring Understanding
Being gifted means different things to different people.

Guiding Question
How are gifted students perceived by friends, teachers, and parents?

A. Have students brainstorm a list of things people expect from gifted children using the categories of teachers, parents and friends. Create a chart on the board.

B. Have students discuss how they feel about these expectations. Why do they think people have these expectations? Have students identify the expectations that they think are reasonable.

C. Have students brainstorm a list of expectations they have for themselves as gifted children. Write the list on the board. Discuss whether or not the expectations are reasonable.

D. Using the list, ask individual students to write a list of what they expect out of themselves. After a few minutes, ask students who expects the most out of them: parents, teachers, friends, or themselves?

E. Have students write a letter to the person who expects the most from them, explaining which expectations are reasonable and which are not. Have students explain in their letter that they know the person wants the best for them, but their expectations are overwhelming at times.

Assessment

Assess the letters from Step E using the rubric on Attachment 2.

Teacher Tip
Rubrics are an effective assessment tool in evaluating student performance in areas that are complex and vague. The rubric by which students will be assessed should be explained before students begin working on an activity or project.

Attachment 2   Friendly Letter Scoring Guide

Name_____ Score _____/18

Content Standard	Standard	Student Assessment	Facilitator Assessment
Letter lists reasonable expectations.	3		
Letter lists unreasonable expectations.	3		
Letter describes how the student feels about the expectations.	3		
Skill Standard			
Letter has an appropriate greeting.	3		
Letter has an opening, body and closing.	3		
Grammar and spelling are accurate.	3		

4= Exceeds standard
3= Meets standard
2= Nearing standard
1= Below standard

14

Activity 3 - I'm Gonna Like ME!

Grades: K - 3

Instructional Materials
- *I'm Gonna Like Me* book, by Jamie Lee Curtis
- drawing paper

> **Enduring Understanding**
> Being gifted means different things to different people.
>
> **Guiding Question**
> How can we celebrate personal differences?

Introduction
Have every student name one thing they like about themselves.

A. Read the story I'm *Gonna Like Me*. Ask students if they would be friends with the girl in the story. Discuss why she would be an interesting person to know.

B. Have students think about things they do that make them happy, but might be considered silly or strange by others.

C. Give students drawing paper folded in half. On the front, have them print "I'm gonna like me. . ." On the inside left, have students write a sentence describing their silly or strange habit or activity. On the inside right, encourage students to draw a picture of what their sentence describes. On the back, have students print their name and date.

I'm
Gonna
Like
Me. . .
by

_____

My mommy has to sing me songs every night before I can go to sleep.

Assessment
Have students share their booklets and tell how they would fit into the story *I'm Gonna Like Me*. Evaluate their understanding of the concept.

Activity 4 - Perception of ME

Grades: 3 - 5

Instructional Materials
- sticky notes

Background Information
Many gifted students have difficulty building self-esteem. Partially this is because we often confuse self-esteem with self image. **Self-esteem** is the importance you place on your ability or inability to do something. **Self-image** is how you perceive yourself doing a task.

Enduring Understanding
Being gifted means different things to different people.

Guiding Question
What is the difference between self esteem and self image?

Introduction
Ask each student to write three things at which they excel on three separate sticky notes. Have students put the sticky notes on the board. Remove any duplicates.

A. Give each student enough sticky notes that they can copy the abilities students listed on the board.

B. Have students prioritize the list from their greatest ability to their greatest disability. Ask students to compare lists and discuss why they think their lists are different from one another.

C. Ask each student to actually do one thing he/she felt good at, and one thing he/she felt worst at in front of the team. Have students describe how they felt in each situation.

D. Have students reflect on how their self-esteem and self-image contributed to how they felt. Ask students to discuss whether it is important to be good at everything.

Assessment
Observe students as they perform in front of the team. Help students understand their feelings and how these relate to self-image and self-esteem.

16

Activity 5 - Fingerprints of Greatness!

Grades: K - 5

Instructional Materials
- copy paper
- markers
- baby wipes
- copies of Attachment 3

Enduring Understanding
Being gifted means different things to different people.

Guiding Question
Who are you as a person?

Preparation
Make the story boards ahead or time by dividing an 8 ½" X 11" piece of typing paper into six equivalent squares. You can make the book pages any size. Using the same size paper as for the story board, cutting it into six separate squares, and making a construction paper cover is recommended.

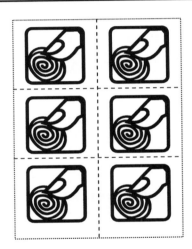

Introduction
Remind students that during the past few lessons they have discovered some of their strengths. Today they will write a story based on their strengths. What makes this activity unique is they will write the story from the perspective of one of their fingers.

A. Using the story board, have students write in the basic idea for each strength they will be describing in their story.

B. Challenge students to write each idea in one or two sentences from their finger's perspective.

C. Give each student a package of markers. Instruct students to color their fingers with the marker of their choice. Have students roll their finger, making a finger print in a story board frame. Have students add details to their fingerprints and create a background.

D. Invite students to share their "Fingerprints of Greatness" stories with the class.

Assessment
Use the rubric on Attachment 3 to evaluate stories.

Name: _____ Score: ___ / 18

Content Standard	Standard	Student Assessment	Facilitator Assessment
Story is from the finger's perspective.	3		
Story tells about the student's personal strength.	3		
Skill Standard			
Each story page has at least one sentence that describes what is happening in the picture.	3		
Finger pictures have details and scenery.	3		
Color is used to enhance the story.	3		
Spelling and grammar is correct.	3		

4= Exceeds standard
3= Meets standard
2= Nearing standard
1= Below standard

UNIT 2

Successful people exhibit the traits of creativity, goal setting, intelligence, courage, and kindness.

Activity 6 - Ready Set Goal

Grade: K - 5

Instructional Materials
- copies of Attachments 4 and 5

Introduction
Ask for three volunteers to do an important job for you. Have the students come to the front of the class. Explain it is very important they follow all directions and complete the job quickly and quietly. Send them to do the job. When students ask what they are to do, remind them to follow directions and complete the job quickly and quietly. Ask the class to state the problem with the directions you have given. (there were none) Ask: Why can't these students be successful? Discuss the need to know where you are going in order to successfully complete a task.

A. Ask students what setting a goal means to them.

B. Have students generate a list of goals they have set and achieved.

C. Tell students they will be setting a goal today. This goal should have the following attributes:
- Your goal should be very specific.
- You need to be able to tell when you have reached the goal.
- You try a new approach to achieving the goal. (People tend to keep using the same strategies, even if they are unsuccessful.)
- You need to set a deadline and stick to it. You can reevaluate your goal at this time.

D. Provide examples of obtainable goals:
- going to college
- scoring a goal in soccer
- learning a dance routine
- getting a better grade on a test
- keeping out of trouble in class or at home

E. Have students write their goal on Attachment 4. These may be displayed in the room.

Assessment
Assess each student's goal using the rubric on Attachment 5.

Enduring Understanding
Successful people exhibit the traits of creativity, goal setting, intelligence, courage, and kindness.

Guiding Question
Why is goal setting important?

Goal
I will have my backpack ready the night before, so I don't have to hurry in the morning.

Steps:
- show my parents what is in the backpack
- do my homework
- return everything to the pack
- place pack by the door

Name: _____

My Goal

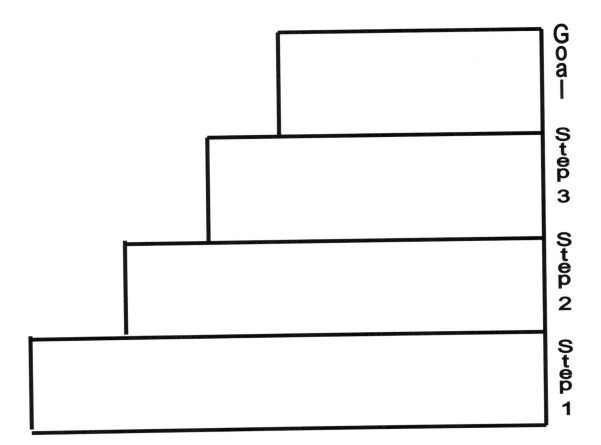

Name _____ Score ____ /12

Content Standard	Standard	Student Assessment	Facilitator Assessment
Student has a logical plan to reach their goal.	3		
Student has identified three steps to meet his/her goal.	3		
Student has a deadline for reaching the goal.	3		
Skill Standard			
Spelling and grammar is correct.	3		

4= Exceeds standard
3= Meets standard
2= Nearing standard
1= Below standard

Activity 7 – WhatsIts?

Grades: 1 – 5

Instructional Materials
- packing peanuts
- toothpicks
- copies of Attachment 6
- Optional: rewards for all students

Enduring Understanding
Successful people exhibit the traits of creativity, goal setting, intelligence, courage, and kindness.

Guiding Question
How are you motivated?
Intrinsically or extrinsically?

Background Information
Learning what motivates students is a valuable activity. This activity demonstrates intrinsic and extrinsic motivators as well as positive and negative reinforcement.

Introduction
Place students in teams of 4-5. Tell students they will be competing against each other in an assembly line competition. You may need to explain the concept of an assembly line to younger children. There will be a reward for the winning team. Avoid telling students what the reward will be. Be sure the teams are separated as you will be giving a different set of instructions to each team.

A. Give each team a set of building materials and a copy of Attachment 6. Tell all teams each student must participate in the building of each WhatsIt. Each WhatsIt is worth 5 points.

B. Tell half of the teams (Motivator A) they need to build as many WhatsIts as they can in the time allotted. They can use the materials in any way they choose as long as the basic shape of the WhatsIt is the same.

C. Tell the other teams (Motivator B) they need to build as many WhatsIts as they can in the time allotted. They will be penalized 2 points for every broken toothpick. Make sure that these teams do not have enough toothpicks to use all of the packing peanuts. They will have to decide whether breaking the toothpicks is worth losing points. (It takes 5 packing peanuts and 8 toothpicks to make 1 WhatsIt.)

D. Give students 8-10 minutes to build the WhatsIts.

E. Provide positive reinforcement to the first teams (Motivator A) by praising their efforts and encouraging them to keep working together. Provide less positive comments such as, "You better hurry up." or "Be careful you don't break anything." to the Motivator B teams.

F. Students will ask what to do when they run out of materials. Restate that they can only use the materials they were given. Let them problem solve. Often students will begin to disagree on what to do, so let them try to figure it out together. You can discuss observed behavior after the activity.

G. At the end of the preset time, ask each team how many complete WhatsIts they made. You may need to check the WhatsIts of younger children for accuracy. Make sure the Motivator B teams deduct 2 points for each toothpick they break.

H. Place all scores on the board keeping the Motivator A teams separate from the Motivator B teams. Generally the Motivator A teams that received positive reinforcement and were told they could break the tooth picks without penalty work more cooperatively and have more WhatsIts. Motivator B teams will feel it was unfair that they were penalized for breaking toothpicks.

I. Ask students in the different teams how they felt during the activity. Discuss why they felt stressed or anxious about not getting the most WhatsIts. Students who were stressed because they wanted to win the reward are extrinsically motivated. Students who are stressed because they just wanted to build the most WhatsIts and feel successful are intrinsically motivated.

J. Ask students why they try to get good grades. Discuss the answers in terms of intrinsic and extrinsic motivators. Explain to students how intrinsic motivation will carry you throughout life, when stickers and candy rewards are no longer offered. Ask students to list extrinsic rewards adults receive. (bonus pay, thank you cards, promotions, etc.)

K. Discuss how well teams worked together. Ask: Did the teams with the positive motivation work more cooperatively than the teams with negative motivation? Why or Why not?

Assessment

Have students either write or express orally why they would help you clean up the room. Have them determine if this is a positive or negative motivator and if they were looking for an extrinsic or intrinsic reward. Older students may be able to relate this to how they are parented. For example, being paid for grades versus being praised.

  extrinsic motivation

Each WhatsIt is made of 5 foam packing peanuts and 8 toothpicks.

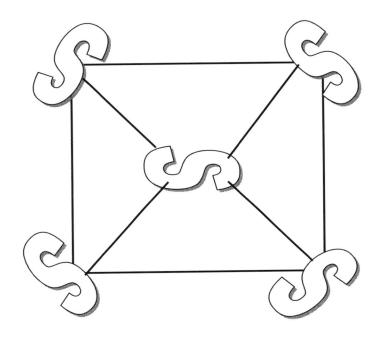

Activity 8 - Recycle ME with FFOE

Grades: K-3

Instructional Materials
- recycled materials
- arts and crafts supplies
- copies of Attachment 7

Enduring Understanding
Successful people exhibit the traits of creativity, goal setting, intelligence, courage, and kindness.

Guiding Question
How are you creative?

Introduction
Ask students to brainstorm what comes to mind when they hear the word tale/tail. Record responses on the board. Tell students fluency describes the number of unique responses they can list. Go over the responses and sort them into categories. Challenge students to look for different ways to think about the homophone tail/tale. Explain that thinking about words in different ways demonstrates flexibility. Ask students to identify the responses they think are most original..

A. Ask students to choose one original response or create another one of their own. Explain to students that they will be elaborating on this idea by adding details.

B. Challenge each student to write a story using their chosen idea. They will also build a character or scene from their story using recycled materials.

C. Have students share their stories and visual products with the class.

D. Discuss how each student used elaboration and creativity in their writing and visual product.

Assessment
Use the rubric on Attachment 7 to evaluate stories and visual products.

Teacher Tip
FFOE is an acronym for fluency, flexibility, originality, and elaboration. This strategy can be used for brainstorming, considering a problem from many angles, etc.

26

Attachment 7   Written and Visual Product

Name _____ Score ___ /18

Content Standard	Standard	Student Assessment	Facilitator Assessment
Story has many details that elaborate on the topic.	3		
Words used in the story paint pictures.	3		
Story has a strong beginning, middle and end.	3		
Character or scene is creatively made with recycled materials.	3		
Skill Standard			
Grammar and spelling is correct.	3		
Story and artwork show student's pride in his/her work.	3		

4= Exceeds standard
3= Meets standard
2= Nearing standard
1= Below standard

27

Activity 9 - Hooray for Diffendoofer Day

Grades: 4 - 5

Instructional Materials
- *Hooray for Diffendoofer Day* book, by Dr. Suess
- arts and crafts supplies
- recycled materials
- copies of Attachment 8

Enduring Understanding
Successful people exhibit the traits of creativity, goal setting, intelligence, courage, and kindness.

Guiding Question
How do creativity and different thinking make learning more enjoyable?

Introduction
Ask students to think about their favorite teacher. Invite students to share one reason they chose that teacher. Have students discuss their favorite way to learn something new.

A. Read *Hooray for Diffendoofer Day*.

B. Ask students why they think the narrator of the story likes Miss Bonkers the best. Discuss how the teachers think differently from one another and use creative ways to teach.

C. Ask: Why do you think the principal established Diffendoofer Day?
Tell students to pretend they are teachers and must teach about a specific topic. (Thanksgiving, volcanoes, immigration) Assign all students the same topic. Challenge students to create the most different and creative way to teach the topic.

D. Have students make their presentations to the class.

E. Discuss how each presentation is creative and different. Encourage students to determine which lessons would have inspired them to learn more about the topic.

Assessment
Use the rubric on Attachment 8 to evaluate lessons.

Extension
Have students write a friendly letter to teachers who taught in different or creative ways, thanking them for great lessons.

Attachment 8   Creative Lesson Presentation

Name _____ Score _____ /15

Content Standard	Standard	Student Assessment	Facilitator Assessment
Lesson was on assigned topic.	3		
Lesson engaged all students in learning.	3		
The creative idea in the lesson was obvious.	3		
Skill Standard			
Presentation was organized and easy to understand.	3		
Student speaks loud enough for everyone to hear.	3		

4= Exceeds standard
3= Meets standard
2= Nearing standard
1= Below standard

Activity 10 - Responsibility and Respect

Grades: K - 3

Instructional Materials
- *I Am Responsible* book, by David Parker
- *I Show Respect* book, by David Parker
- *I'm in Charge of Me* book, by David Parker
- copies of Attachments 9 and 10

Enduring Understanding
Successful people exhibit the traits of creativity, goal setting, intelligence, courage, and kindness.

Guiding Question
How can gifted children show responsibility and respect for others?

Introduction
Ask students to define responsibility and respect. Record responses on the board, separating the responses to make a Venn diagram. Ask students if any of their responses are the same between the two words. Place those responses in the center. Tell students at the end of the activity, they will revisit these ideas and see if they feel the same way about the definitions.

A. Read *I Am Responsible*. Ask students to make a list of the things they are responsible for doing each day. Have students share three things from their lists. Discuss the consequences of not performing these tasks. Ask students what would happen if different workers (bus drivers, doctors, grocers) refused to do their jobs. Allow time for discussion.

B. Read *I Show Respect*. Make a chart on the board with the following headings: Me, My Family, My Friends, Other People. Reread each page in the story and ask students to identify who the character is respecting. Place a tally mark in the appropriate column in your chart. Ask students to list other ways they show respect and place a tally mark in the appropriate column in the chart. Discuss the distribution of tally marks. Explain that their behavior impacts themselves and others.

C. Read *I'm in Charge of Me*. Have students list the choices they make in the morning before school. For example:
*what to wear   *what to eat for breakfast   *whether or not to watch T.V.

D. Ask students to think about the last time they felt bored. What choices could they have made to change how they felt?

E. Have students make a cartoon panel using Attachment 9. Pictures should be in color and captions should describe what they could do to break boredom.

Assessment
Use the rubric on Attachment 10 to evaluate cartoons.

30

Name_____

31

Attachment 10   Cartoon- "When I feel bored..."

Name_____ Score____/15

Content Standard	Standard	Student Assessment	Facilitator Assessment
Cartoon describes at least three things a student could do to break boredom.	3		
Pictures are related to the way boredom can be broken.	3		
Skill Standard			
Grammar and spelling are correct.	3		
Pictures are in color.	3		
Captions are in complete sentences at the bottom of the picture or in speech bubbles	3		

4= Exceeds standard
3= Meets standard
2= Nearing standard
1= Below standard

Activity 11 - Put Your Best Foot Forward

Grades: 1 - 3

Instructional Materials
- copies of Attachment 11
- empty cereal boxes
- masking, packing or duct tape
- ribbon, flowers, feathers, pompons, buttons, etc

Introduction
Ask students if they have ever been uncomfortable meeting new adults or talking to their teacher about a problem in school. Explain that how they behave when they meet new adults and how they talk to people when they have a problem influences the way an adult feels about them. We call this making an impression on someone. You can make a good impression or a bad impression. Remind students that it takes a little courage and practice to make a good impression.

A. Choose one student as a volunteer. Explain that you will pretend to meet the student for the first time. Go up to the student, introduce yourself, and shake hands. Ask the students what they noticed about this staged meeting. Explain that to make a good impression is easy. Review how to make a good impression using the steps in the box.

B. Role-play meeting each student and ask them a few questions about themselves. Have students critique the meetings.

C. Ask students to brainstorm a list of reasons they might need to talk to the teacher about a problem. Have a volunteer present the problem to you. Critique the presentation and tell students that prior preparation makes a presentation easier.

> ### Enduring Understanding
> Successful people exhibit the traits of creativity, goal setting, intelligence, courage, and kindness.
>
> ### Guiding Question
> How can gifted students exhibit courage?

> ## How to Make a Good Impression
>
> - Look the adult in the eye.
> - Introduce yourself in a clear voice that is loud enough to hear.
> - Restate the name of the person you just met. Ex: It's nice to meet you Mrs. Brown.
> - Always say "please" and "thank you" and say "yes" or "no" instead of "yeah" and "nope".

D. Choose a situation, have students form small teams, and have them practice preparing to talk to a teacher given the following instructions:

- Make an appointment to meet. Sometimes the teacher is too busy to talk immediately, so making an appointment shows you respect the teacher's time and that you are serious about the problem.
- See if anyone else in your class feels the same way as you do. When more people have a concern, an adult may be more likely to pay attention.
- Write down what you want to talk about. You can even give it to your teacher ahead of time, so they have time to think about the concern.
- Choose your words carefully. Avoid words like boring, stupid, etc.
- Offer solutions to the problem. If you do not want to write another book report, provide some things you would do, such as create a commercial about the book.
- Be respectful.
- Focus on your need without blaming the teacher or anyone in your class.
- Listen carefully without interrupting.

E. Invite a colleague or principal to come and have the students present a different concern to them. Have the adults give feedback based on their presentation.

F. Have students make a pair of cereal box sandals using the instructions on Attachment 11 to remind them how to put their best foot forward with adults.

Assessment

Observe students during role playing and make note of students who could use extra coaching. Look at the sandals and see which tip(s) each student thought would help them most.

Notes

_____

_____

_____

_____

_____

_____

_____

_____

_____

_____

34

Attachment 11   Cereal Box Sandals

1.   Have each student stand on an open, flattened cereal box and trace around his/her shoe.

2.   Cut out shoe and as many straps as the student wants (1-3).

3.   Tape the straps in place. For the best fit, wrap and tape the straps and soles together on the student's bare feet.

4.   Students may decorate the sandals any way they like.

5.   Students should write at least 1 tip for talking with adults on the bottom of each sandal using a permanent marker.

Activity 12 - No Fear

Grades: 4 - 5

Instructional Materials
- poster board
- markers or paint
- copies of Attachments 12 and 13

Introduction
Have students define courage. Tell students

courage is taking action in spite of being afraid. Explain that people with courage are willing to take thoughtful risks to accomplish something worthwhile. Stress that people should not take foolish risks in a situation where there is no chance for success. Risks may be physical, mental, social or financial.

A. Invite students to tell about a time they took a thoughtful risk. Discuss how they felt before and after the event.

B. Have students share examples of things they would be afraid to do. (walk around in the dark, speak in front of the class) Help students determine whether these risks are thoughtful or foolish. Discuss what steps they could take to make the risk less frightening. (a flashlight in the dark, a helmet when you skateboard)

C. Explain that warriors in many cultures carried shields or banners to display their courage and communicate something about them. Show students pictures of Native American shields, European crests, and Japanese banners. Explain the significance of the animals and colors.

D. Have students design a banner or shield that represents them and one act of courage they have accomplished. Provide copies of Attachment 12 for instructions.

E. Have students share their shields or banners with the class. Invite students to discuss why it is important to be courageous on occasion.

Assessment
Use the rubric on Attachment 13 to evaluate the banners and shields.

Name _____

There are three major parts of a banner or a shield that reveal a person's heraldry. Heraldry is a visual language originally used to identify knights.

The surface of the shield or banner can be divided into parts or "**fields**". These fields symbolize parts of someone's personality or feats of bravery they have performed.

The **charge** is a symbol or picture that represents trait or object.

The **tincture** refers to the colors used on the banner or shield. The rules of tincture state that no metal should be placed next to another metal (gold, silver) and no color should be placed next to another color. Even the colors have meanings.

> White/silver- faith and purity
> Yellow/gold- honor and loyalty
> Black- grief or anger
> Purple- royalty, passion or suffering
> Blue- tenacity and religious
> Green- youth and health

1. Describe yourself in three words.

    a.

    b.

    c.

2. Describe an act of courage you have accomplished.

3. How many fields will you need to represent yourself and your act of courage?

4. What colors can you use to represent yourself and your courageous act?

5. What charges will you place in your fields to represent yourself and your courageous act?

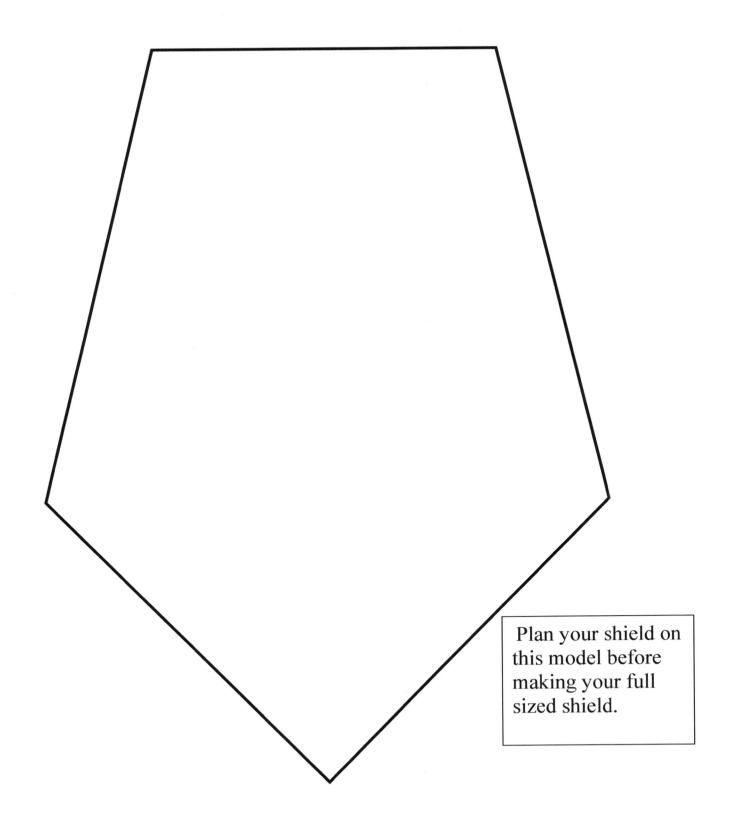

Plan your shield on this model before making your full sized shield.

Use this banner
to plan before
you make your
full sized
banner.

Name _____ Score _____ /21

Content Standard	Standard	Student Assessment	Facilitator Assessment
Shield or banner represents the student.	3		
Shield or banner represents the student's act of courage.	3		
Shield or banner has logical fields.	3		
Shield or banner follows the rules of tincture.	3		
Shield or banner uses appropriate charges to represent the student.	3		
Skill Standard			
Shield or banner is in color.	3		
Shield or banner shows student pride in his/her work.	3		

4= Exceeds standard

3= Meets standard

2= Nearing standard

1= Below standard

Activity 13 - It's Okay to Be Different

Grades: K - 3

Instructional Materials

- *I Accept You As You Are* book, by David Parker
- *It's Okay to Be Different* book, by Todd Parr
- large drawing paper
- markers or crayons

Enduring Understanding
Successful people exhibit the traits of creativity, goal setting, intelligence, courage, and kindness.

Guiding Question
How do people's differences make the world a richer place to live?

Introduction
Read *I Accept You As You Are* and allow time for discussion.

A. Have students list 5 ways they are the same as all the others in their class. (ten fingers, breathe air, can talk) Encourage students to list 5 ways they are different from others in their class. (name, physical appearance, pet's name)

B. Ask students what they think is more important: the similarities or the differences. Ask: Which makes the world more interesting, the similarities or the differences between people?

C. Read *It's Okay to Be Different*. Ask students to think about what is different about them that others do not know.

D. Have students draw a picture of how they are different and have them write a caption starting with, "It's okay……" Use the large drawing paper for this part of the activity.

E. Have students share their drawings. Explain that these differences add richness and uniqueness to our lives and are not reasons to dislike one another.

Assessment
Observe the discussion and view the students' drawings to see if they understood the value of differences.

Activity 14 - Don't Laugh At Me

Grades: 4 - 5

Instructional Materials
- *Don't Laugh At Me* book ,by Steve Seskin and Allen Shamblin

Introduction
Invite a speaker with a disability to come to your class. Someone who is in a wheelchair or who is deaf would be a good choice.

Enduring Understanding
Successful people exhibit the traits of creativity, goal setting, intelligence, courage, and kindness.

Guiding Question
How can we treat people with disabilities with respect?

A. Have students listen to the speaker and ask questions about what it is like to have a disability.

B. Read *Don't Laugh At Me*.

C. Have students listen to the song "Don't Laugh At Me" in the back of the book. Ask students what the author means by the last line of the chorus.

D. Ask students to think of a way they are disabled (cannot dance, cannot ride a bike, poor vision).

E. Have students describe times when they have or have seen others make fun of someone else. Discuss why they think people make fun of others or stare at them.

F. Have students devise positive ways to act around people with disabilities. Have students form pairs and role-play these new behaviors.

Assessment
Observe student responses.

43

Activity 15 - I Pledge

Grades: K - 5

Instructional Materials
- copies of Attachments 14 and 15
- drawing paper

Introduction

Challenge students to discuss the meaning of the
Pledge of Allegiance. Distribute copies of the
Pledge of Allegiance. Review each line and have students look up the unfamiliar words
until you have rewritten the pledge in understandable language. Ask students how their
understanding of the pledge has changed.

A. Tell students they will be writing a class pledge. Distribute copies of Attachment 14.
Have students list all the things they are willing to do under each category.

B. Invite students to share their responses. Record responses on the board under each
category. Do not repeat an item on the list.

C. Remind students the pledge cannot be a class pledge unless everyone agrees on each
item. Have students close their eyes. As you read each item say, "If you are NOT willing
to do (item) raise your hand." If anyone raises their hand, erase that item from the list.
Continue through the whole list.

D. Have students open their eyes. They are usually surprised at how many items were
removed. Divide the remaining items between students and have them draw a
picture with a caption for each item they pledge as a class. One student should
make the title page.

E. Laminate the drawings and create a book. Consider reciting your pledge
every class meeting.

Assessment
Observe students as they give responses.

Enduring Understanding
Successful people exhibit the traits
of creativity, goal setting,
intelligence, courage, and kindness.

Guiding Question
How can gifted students show
regard for others on a daily basis?

44

Attachment 14	Pledges

Name: _____

Pledges I can keep towards my family:

Pledges I can keep towards my friends:

Pledges I can keep at school:

Pledges I can keep to help the environment:

I pledge allegiance

to the flag

of the United States of America

and to the republic

for which it stands

one nation, under God,

indivisible

with liberty and justice

for all.

Activity 16 - Caught in the Act

Grades: K - 3

Instructional Materials
- *I Am Generous* book, by David Parker
- *Kids' Random Acts of Kindness* book, Foreword by Rosalynn Carter and Introduction by Dawna Markova
- large drawing paper
- markers or crayons
- copies of Attachments 16 and 17

Enduring Understanding
Successful people exhibit the traits of creativity, goal setting, intelligence, courage, and kindness.

Guiding Question
How can gifted students show regard for others on a daily basis?

Introduction
Read *I Am Generous*.

A. Have students brainstorm ways they could be generous.

B. Give each student drawing paper and have them create wanted posters for kind or generous behavior. Ask them how we could use the posters to increase generosity in their school.

C. Place students in small teams and have them write an action plan using Attachment 16. Have teams share their action plans and encourage the class to choose the plan they wish to follow.

D. Carry out the chosen plan.

E. Read selections from the Kid's Random Acts of Kindness. Ask students to relate some random acts of kindness they have done or witnessed. Discuss how they felt about the act of kindness.

F. Challenge students to do one act of kindness or generosity every day.

Assessment
Evaluate action plans using the rubric on Attachment 17.

Name_____

Step #1- List some ideas for being generous at school.

Step #2- Choose one idea to develop and list it below.

Step #3- List all the possible ways you could implement your idea at school.

Step #4- Choose one of the implementation ideas and list all of the possible problems you might have implementing it at school.

Step #5- What adults at your school will you need to involve in implementing your idea?

Step #6- List the things you will need to do to prepare for implementation of your idea.

Step # 7- What materials will you need to complete the plan?

Attachment 17 Generosity Action Plan Rubric

Name_____ Score_____/18

Content Standard	Standard	Student Assessment	Facilitator Assessment
Idea for generosity could be implemented.	3		
All problems with implementation are thought out.	3		
Appropriate adults are listed in implementation.	3		
A list of things needed to implement the idea is thorough.	3		
All materials needed for implementation are listed.	3		
Skill Standard			
I worked cooperatively in the team.	3		

4= Exceeds standard
3= Meets standard
2= Nearing standard
1= below standard

Activity 17 - You're Mean

Grades: 4 - 5

Instructional Materials
- one large cut out heart per student
- copies of Attachment 18

Introduction
Give each student a large cut out heart. Have them write their name in the center.

A. Have each student recall and share something negative they have heard about themselves. As each negative thing is said have every student crumple a small piece of their paper heart. At the end the entire heart should be crumpled.

B. Invite each student to recall and share something positive they have heard about themselves. As each positive thing is said have every student uncrumple a small piece of their paper heart. At the end the entire heart should be uncrumpled.

C. Discuss how hearts are still scarred by mean words no matter how many kind things you hear. Ask students which do they remember more, negative comments or positive comments. Why?

Assessment
Challenge students to write a paragraph from a heart's perspective about mean words. Have them title it "You're breaking My Heart".

Use the rubric on Attachment 18 to evaluate writing.

Name: _____ Score ___/15

Content Standard	Standard	Student Assessment	Facilitator Assessment
Paragraph was from a heart's point of view.	3		
Paragraph relates how mean words hurt.	3		
Skill Standard			
Spelling and grammar are correct.	3		
Story has a clear beginning, middle and end.	3		
Story makes sense.	3		

4= Exceeds standard
3= Meets standard
2= Nearing standard
1= Below standard

UNIT 3

A person who chooses a career based on his or her intelligences may be more productive and satisfied in his or her career.

Activity 18 - Multiple What?

Grades: K - 5

Instructional Materials
- computer with Internet access
- one coat hanger per student
- small squares of paper, 3" x 3"
- string or yarn
- copies of Attachment 20

Enduring Understanding
A person who chooses a career based on his or her intelligences may be more productive and satisfied in his or her career.

Guiding Question
What multiple intelligences do you have?

Introduction
Ask students to name one thing at which they excel.

A. List the responses on the board and discuss what type of knowledge a person needs to excel at that particular activity.

B. Explain that there are nine multiple intelligences: visual /spatial, verbal/linguistic, mathematical/logical, bodily/kinesthetic, musical/rhythmic, intrapersonal, interpersonal, naturalist and existentialist. See Attachment 19 for an explanation of each intelligence.

C. Help students match the activity they are good at with the intelligence the activity describes.

D. Visit the following Web site and allow students to take the Multiple Intelligences Inventory. As always, please preview all sites before allowing student access.
http://surfaquarium.com/MI/inventory.htm

E. Have students complete and score the inventory.

F. Have students create a mobile of their intelligences. Make sure their name and/or photo is at the top of the mobile. Hang mobiles in the room for the next activity.

Assessment
Use the rubric on Attachment 20 to evaluate mobiles.

Visual/Spatial- Children who learn best visually and organize things spatially are considered visual/spatial. These children like to see what you are talking about. They enjoy charts, graphs, maps, tables, illustrations, art, puzzles and costumes.

Verbal/Linguistic- Children who are strong in speaking, writing, reading and listening are considered verbal/linguistic. They tend to be successful in the traditional classroom.

Mathematical/Logical- Children who have an aptitude for numbers and problem solving are considered mathematical/logical. These children also do well in a traditional classroom.

Bodily/Kinesthetic- Children who are considered bodily/kinesthetic learn best through activities like games, movement, hands-on and building. These children are often seen as overly active in the traditional classroom where they must sit still.

Musical/Rhythmic- Children who learn better through songs, patterns, rhythms, instruments and musical expression are considered musical/rhythmic.

Intrapersonal- Children considered to have intrapersonal intelligence are in touch with their own feelings, values and ideas. They often appear reserved but are quite intuitive.

Interpersonal- Children considered to have interpersonal intelligence are outgoing, work well in cooperative teams or with a partner. These children are generally talkative and social.

Naturalist- Children with naturalist intelligence love the outdoors, animals and field trips. These children pick up the subtle differences in meanings.

Existentialist- An existentialist child learns in the context of how they fit in the big picture of existence. These children are more philosophical.

Attachment 20　　　　　　　　　　　　Mobile

Name_____ Score_____ /18

Content Standard	Standard	Student Assessment	Facilitator Assessment
My name and photo is at the top of the mobile.	3		
The mobile displays my multiple intelligences with pictures.	3		
The mobile displays my multiple intelligences with words.	3		
Skill Standard			
Mobile is constructed well and is suitable for hanging in the classroom.	3		
Spelling on the mobile is correct.	3		
Pictures are large enough to see with the mobiles hanging and are in color.	3		

4= Exceeds standard
3= Meets standard
2= Nearing standard
1= Below standard

Activity 19 - Which Hat For ME?

Grades: K - 3

Instructional Materials
- hats for various careers
- copies of Attachments 21, 22, and 23

Introduction
Show students a variety of hats. Ask them to identify the career each hat represents. Ask students which hat they would choose for their future career. If a career is not represented, ask students to describe what the hat might look like. Discuss the importance of thinking about future careers.

> **Enduring Understanding**
> A person who chooses a career based on his or her intelligences may be more productive and satisfied in his or her career.
>
> **Guiding Question**
> Which career best suits your intelligences?

A. Have students choose a career they think they would enjoy. Have students research the career and find three facts about the responsibilities of the job.

B. Give each student a copy of Attachment 21. Tell students to cut apart the icons. Read a description of each of the multiple intelligences to students and explain how each icon represents that intelligence.

C. Invite students to look at the facts about their jobs and determine which intelligences they would need for that job. Have each student justify his or her choices. Have students paste their chosen intelligences to Attachment 22.
Have each student make a hat. See Attachment 23 for instructions.

D. During the next class session, have students paint and decorate their hats. Decorations should reflect the intelligences needed for their career.

E. Have students present their hats and careers to the class.

Assessment
Ask students to compare their My Career Hat sheets to their mobiles. Discuss how successful they might be in their careers based on their intelligences. Discuss the idea of improving in an area in which they are lacking.

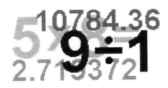

Name_____

My chosen career is _____.
Three facts about my responsibilities in my chosen career are:

1.

2.

3.

The intelligences I would need for my job are:

The reasons I chose these intelligences are:

Materials needed:
- large craft paper
- papier-mâché or wall paper paste
- cereal bowls or empty cool whip tubs
- string
- newspaper
- tempera paint
- decorations

Directions: (Make hats on a table covered in plastic or paper.)

1. Fold a large piece of craft paper in half.
2. Spread papier-mâché on the paper. (Paste should be soupy.)
3. Center the folded paper over the upside down bowl or tub.
4. Mold paper around the bowl.
5. Tie a piece of string around the bowl near the table to form the brim of the hat.
6. Trim the edges to make the brim any size you want.
7. Dip newspaper strips in the papier-mâché one at a time, removing extra paste by running each strip between your thumb and finger.
8. Place strips over crown and brim of hat to make it stronger.
9. Let hat dry. When dry, paint and decorate.

Activity 20 – Lifestyle Choices and Career Choices

Grades: 4 - 5

Instructional Materials
- computer with Internet access
- reference materials on various careers
- copies of Attachments 24 and 25
- calculators

Introduction
Ask students why people choose certain careers. Is it a passionate interest or the promise of big money? Discuss whether or not it would be better to choose how you want to live and try to obtain it through a career or should you choose a career you would love even if you could not live in a big house and drive a fancy car.

> ### Enduring Understanding
> A person who chooses a career based on his or her intelligences may be more productive and satisfied in his or her career.
>
> ### Guiding Question
> Should your career choice be based on its ability to support the lifestyle of your choice? Should you choose a career based on passion or on potential earnings?

A. Distribute copies of Attachment 24. Have students select a house and a car using the internet or the local paper. The following Web sites may be helpful. As always, please preview all sites before allowing student access.

Web sites for homes:
www.realtor.com
www.Homeseekers.com
www.century21.com
www.homebuilder.com

Web sites for vehicles:
www.autoweb.com
www.autotrader.com

B. Allow students to use calculators to make the calculations on the worksheet. Have students look through the reference materials and choose a career about which they could be passionate. Help students discover the average salary for that career. Here are some Web sites that may help with this research.
www.bls.gov/oco/ocoiab.htm   **www.salaryexpert.com**

C. Have students compare their chosen salary with their lifestyle costs on the worksheet. If they are unable to finance their lifestyle ask them to change their job, their house or their car, until they can afford their lifestyle.

D. Discuss what they had to change and how they felt about the choices they had to make.

Assessment
Have students write a paragraph revisiting the question whether or not it would be better to choose how you want to live and try to obtain it through a career or should you choose a career you would love even if you could not live in a big house and drive a fancy car?
Evaluate the activity using the rubric on Attachment 25.

Attachment 24   Can I Afford My Lifestyle?

Name_____

1. Using either real estate Web site, choose a city in which to live and then choose a house.

_____ Purchase price

2. Using the loan calculator, determine what your house payment would be per month.

_____ monthly house payment

_____ yearly house payment (monthly X 12)

3. Using either car Web site, choose a car.

_____Make _____Model

_____Purchase price

4. Using the loan calculator, determine what your car payment would be per month.

_____ monthly car payment

_____ yearly car payment

5. Using the career website or other available resources, choose a career you could be passionate about.

My chosen career is _____.

My average yearly salary will be _____.

My average monthly salary will be _____.
        (yearly salary divided by 12)

6. Take your average salary X .40 this is the amount of your income you should be spending on a car and house payment per month.

The money I should spend on my house and car payment is

$_____.

7. Add the monthly house payment   _____

  to the monthly car payment   + _____

             Total payment= _____

8.Compare your total payment calculated in #7 to the monthly salary calculated in #5. If your answer in #7 is larger than your answer in #5, you need to change your house or car or career choice, re-calculate and compare the totals again.

Name _____ Score_____/15

Content Standard	Standard	Student Assessment	Facilitator Assessment
Ideas relate to the topic of career versus lifestyle.	3		
My opinion is clear to the reader.	3		
Skill Standard			
Paragraph has a clear beginning, middle and end.	3		
Spelling and grammar is correct.	3		
Writing is neat and pride is shown in the final draft.	3		

4= Exceeds standard
3= Meets standard
2= Nearing standard
1= Below standard

UNIT 4

Understanding why people tease others may allow you to choose how to deal with teasing.

Activity 21 - You Can't Bug ME!

Grades: K - 3

Instructional Materials
- *Chrysanthemum* book, by Kevin Henke
- note cards
- drawing paper or recyclable material

Introduction
Distribute a note card to each student. Have them print their name on the card. Ask students to tell something they notice about their name. (Mary – has a "y" at the end that sounds like "e") Have students share what they noticed about their names.

A. Read *Chrysanthemum*.

B. Ask students why they think people tease others (jealousy, low self esteem, they don't like you, just for fun). Explain that they may not be able to stop someone from teasing them, but they can control how they respond.

C. Ask students to identify the following from the story:
- Who is doing the teasing?
- Why are they teasing?
- Was teasing accepted?
- How did the mouse overcome teasing?

D. Tell students there are four things they can do when someone teases them.
- Take a deep breath to relax
- Stand straight and tall
- Tell the person teasing you how you feel
- Ask for an apology or walk away

E. Write the name "Chrysanthemum" on the board and ask students what they can see in her name. Compare these answers with the observations they made about their own names. Discuss how a name is just letters and doesn't define a person. Many people have the same name, but the people are different.

Enduring Understanding
Understanding why people tease others may allow you to choose how to deal with teasing.

Guiding Question
Why do people tease each other?
What should you do when you are teased?

F. Tell students they will make an anti-teasing bug using their names. They are to use the first letter of their name and add details to turn it into a bug. Provide drawing paper or allow them to make 3D models of their anti-teasing name bugs. Remind students to think about the wonder of their name and how it represents a unique person the next time someone teases them.

Assessment

Have students share their bugs and tell one thing they will do the next time someone teases them.

Notes

_____

_____

_____

_____

_____

_____

_____

_____

_____

_____

_____

_____

_____

_____

_____

_____

_____

_____

_____

_____

UNIT 5

Stress is in our everyday lives. Learning to recognize personal stressors may allow you to diffuse stress appropriately.

Activity 22 - I'm Stressed Out

Grades: 4 - 5

Instructional Materials
- copies of Attachment 26

Introduction
Make a list of all your responsibilities each day on the board for the class. Tell them these things can cause us stress

Enduring Understanding
Stress is in our everyday lives. Learning to recognize personal stressors may allow you to diffuse stress appropriately.

Guiding Question
What types of things cause you stress? How can I make my problems solvable?

because we are all pulled in many directions each day by our responsibilities. This can make us feel "stressed out". Tell students that they will discover which items stress them the most and what they can do to lessen stress in the areas listed.

A. Distribute copies of Attachment 26.

B. Have students rank the list of activities and responsibilities. From the ranking have students create a pie graph to reflect their stressors. Then, have students create a pie graph of how they would like their life to be.

C. Have students answer the reflective questions.
- What item on your list got the most stressor votes?
- Why is that item so stressful for you?
- Which item on your list got the least stressor votes?
- Why do you find this least stressful?
- When looking at your graph of how you would like your life to look, which area would you change the most?
- How could you change this item?
- What obstacles are there for you to change this item?
- Who could help you overcome these obstacles?

Assessment
Students should present one change they would like to make in their daily lives based on the activity. Use the rubric on Attachment 27 to evaluate this activity.

Name _____

You have ten votes to use between the 6 choices below. You can divide the votes anyway you want. Make sure that you give the most votes to the thing that stresses you most. When you add up all of your votes, you should only have a total of 10.

_____   Family

_____   School/ Homework

_____   Friends

_____   Chores

_____   After-school activities

_____   Other - _____

Now, complete the table below.

Stressor	Number of Votes	Percent of the Total (# votes/10 X 100)	Degrees of the Circle (% X 360)/100
Family			
School/homework			
Friends			
Chores			
After-school Activities			
Other-			

Using your protractor and the data in the degrees of the circle column of the table, make a pie graph of your stressors.

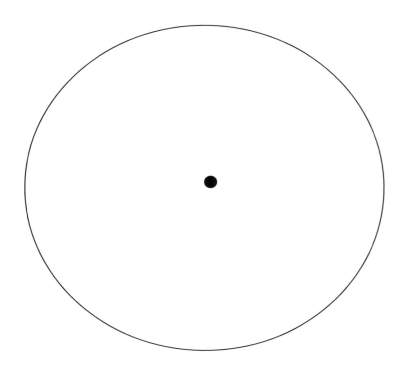

Now make a pie graph of how you would like your life to look.

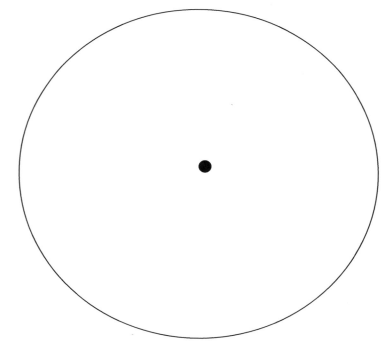

Attachment 27		Oral Communication	

Name _____ Score_____ /18

Content Standard	Standard	Student Assessment	Facilitator Assessment
I can clearly explain why some people are perfectionists.	3		
I can clearly explain why perfectionism is not always good.	3		
I can clearly explain my personal opinion on perfectionism.	3		
Skill Standard			
I had good eye contact with the audience.	3		
I had good volume during my presentation.	3		
My speech is makes sense and has a logical order.	3		

4= Exceeds standard
3= Meets standard
2= Nearing standard
1= Below standard

Activity 23 - Adrenalin

Grades: 3 -4

Instructional Materials
- *Stress Can Really Get On Your Nerves* book, by Trevor Romain & Elizabeth Verdick
- drawing paper

Enduring Understanding
Stress is in our everyday lives. Learning to recognize personal stressors may allow you to diffuse stress appropriately.

Guiding Question
How does your body react to stress?

Introduction
Role-play a stressful situation, like having to sing in front of a large audience. Describe how you are feeling both emotionally and physically.

A. Have students brainstorm how they feel when they are stressed. List their responses on the board.

B. Explain that our bodies actually change physically when we are stressed. This is due to a hormone called adrenalin, which controls our fight or flight response.·

C. Ask students what physical changes they notice when they are stressed or afraid. Possible answers include:
- heart beats faster so you can run or defend yourself
- blood rushes to your muscles in your arms and legs
- you begin to sweat
- your stomach shuts down
- your mouth gets dry
- your hands and feet get colder
- your mind goes blank

D. Have students draw a picture of a stressful feeling from the list they brainstormed. Ask them to include one of the physical changes in their drawing as well.

Assessment
Have students describe how stressful emotions are combined with physical reactions as they share their drawings with the class. Observe how well students understand the relationship between stressful emotions and physical reactions.

72

Activity 24 - Stress Busters

Grades: 1 - 3

Instructional Materials
- *Stress Can Really Get On Your Nerves* book, by Trevor Romain & Elizabeth Verdick
- copies of Attachments 28 and 29

Introduction
Ask students if they think of themselves as fragile. Ask students to brainstorm ways we protect our bodies from damage. (helmet, seatbelt)

Enduring Understanding
Stress is in our everyday lives. Learning to recognize personal stressors may allow you to diffuse stress appropriately.

Guiding Question
How can you reduce stress?

A. Challenge students to define stress. Explain that stress makes us fragile by causing our bodies to react in a way that can be hard on them. Have students brainstorm ways to describe how they feel when they are stressed.

B. Have students choose the descriptions that relate to physical reactions of the body and then help them add more.

C. Have students brainstorm sources of stress. Tell them everyone has some stress, but it is how we deal with stress that matters.

D. Have students choose 5 things that stress them from the brainstormed list. Challenge them to write about a way they could defeat that stressor. (If you are restless, you could go for a walk.)

E. Have students create a booklet on stress busters or write and perform a short play on beating stress.

Assessment
Use the rubrics on Attachments 28 and 29 to evaluate this activity.

Attachment 28 — Stress Busters Booklet

Name_____ Score_____ / 18

Content Standard	Standard	Student Assessment	Facilitator Assessment
Booklet has at least 5 things that stress you.	3		
Each stressor has an idea to beat stress.	3		
Each stressor/ stress buster has an illustration.	3		
Skill Standard			
Grammar and spelling is accurate.	3		
Booklet has a clear beginning, middle and end.	3		
Artwork is neat and in color.	3		

4= Exceeds standard
3= Meets standard
2= Nearing standard
1= Below standard

Attachment 29   Stress Busters Play

Name_____ Score____ / 18

Content Standard	Standard	Student Assessment	Facilitator Assessment
Play has at least 5 things that stress you.	3		
Each stressor has an idea to beat stress.	3		
Each stressor/ stress buster has a prop.	3		
Skill Standard			
Grammar and spelling is accurate.	3		
Play has a clear beginning, middle and end.	3		
Props are neat and enhance the play.	3		

4= Exceeds standard
3= Meets standard
2= Nearing standard
1= Below standard

UNIT 6

We experience a range of emotions everyday. Identifying emotions, especially anger, may help you cope with daily situations. Anger is a normal emotion – how you deal with your anger is a choice.

Activity 25 - Today I Feel Silly

Grades: K - 5

Instructional Materials

- *Today I Feel Silly* book, by Jamie Lee Curtis
- copies of Attachment 30
- construction paper

Introduction
Read *Today I Feel Silly*.

Enduring Understanding
We experience a range of emotions everyday. Identifying emotions, especially anger, may help you cope with daily situations. Anger is a normal emotion – how you deal with your anger is a choice.

Guiding Question
What are my various emotions?
What emotions do you experience in everyday situations?

A. Reread the book and have students name every emotion mentioned. Record the emotions on the board.

B. Put students into pairs. Have students make the face for each emotion listed on the board to each other. Distribute copies of Attachment 30.

C. Have students write the name of each emotion under one of the ovals. Tell students to draw the facial expression for each emotion. Remind them each picture needs to look different.

D. Have students cut off the title of the Attachment and mount their work on a piece of construction paper. Title the construction paper, Today I feel…….

E. Have students cut out a construction paper frame to add to their chart. Have students frame the emotion they are feeling currently.

Assessment
Give students the following situations and have students indicate on their "Today I feel" chart the emotion the situation evokes.
- Your friend refuses to talk to you and won't tell you why he/she is mad.
- You open your front door and your favorite celebrity is standing there.
- You have to sit still for a very long time at an adult function.
- You are wearing unmatched clothes and a large hat.

Name _____

Activity 26 - I'm So Angry

Grades: K - 5

Instructional Materials
- *Alexander and the Terrible, Horrible, No Good, Very Bad Day* book, by Judith Viorst
- copies of the pamphlet, What To Do When I'm Angry
- copies of Attachment 2 from Activity 2

Enduring Understanding
We experience a range of emotions everyday. Identifying emotions, especially anger, may help you cope with daily situations. Anger is a normal emotion – how you deal with your anger is a choice.

Guiding Question
What things make you angry?
How can you handle the emotion of anger?

Preparation
Go to the following Web address to download a copy of the pamphlet, What To Do When I'm Angry.
www.childrenshealthfund.org

Introduction
Ask students to name things and or situations that make them angry. Write the list on half the board. See if students can categorize the things that make them angry.

A. Read *Alexander and the Terrible, Horrible, No Good, Very Bad Day*.

B. Reread the story and at the end of each page have students identify the things that made Alexander angry. List these on the other half of the board.

C. Invite students to compare the lists.

D. Give students the pamphlet What To Do When I'm Angry. Discuss positive ways to deal with anger.

Have students write Alexander a friendly letter giving him a tip for dealing with three situations in the story that made Alexander angry.

Assessment
Use the rubric on Attachment 2 to evaluate letters.

79

UNIT 7

Making and keeping friends may help alleviate stress.

Activity 27 - Qualities of Friends

Grades: K - 1

Instructional Materials

- *Do You Want to Be My Friend?* book, by Eric Carle
- *I'm a Good Friend* book, by David Parker
- washable finger paint
- large drawing paper

> **Enduring Understanding**
> Making and keeping friends may help alleviate stress.
>
> **Guiding Question**
> How do you make a friend?

Preparation

Use note cards and string to create a necklace for each student. On each note card, write the name of a hobby, or a pleasant personality trait.

Introduction

Give each student a necklace. Have students look at the cards and decide whom they would choose to befriend. Discuss how and why they made their choices.

A. Have students brainstorm a list of qualities they look for in a friend.

B. Share the book *Do You Want to Be My Friend?* Ask students what they think the mouse was looking for in a friend? Why did the other animals not want to be his friend?

C. Read *I'm a Good Friend.* Discuss the qualities of friends mentioned in the story. Reread the story if necessary.

D. Have students list five reasons they think they would be a good friend. Have them rank the reasons 1-5 with 1 being their best quality as a friend.

E. Students will be making friendship circles. Have each child make a handprint with washable finger paint on a piece of drawing paper. After the paintings have dried, have students use a black Sharpie to write their qualities over their hand prints on each painting. Have students sit in a circle to share their good qualities.

F. Discuss with students how we choose different types of people to be our friends. Explain how this fills our lives and makes them richer.

Assessment

Observe students choices when choosing friends in the introduction activity.

Activity 28 - Why Do We Need Friends?

Grades: 2 - 3

Instructional Materials
- *Stevie* book, by John Steptoe
- construction paper
- markers or paint

Enduring Understanding
Making and keeping friends may help alleviate stress.

Guiding Question
How do you keep a friend?

Introduction
Ask students why they need friends. Record their responses on the board.

A. Read *Stevie*.

B. Discuss the activities Stevie and Robert do together.

C. Ask students how Stevie feels about Robert while he is living with Stevie and after Robert moves away.

D. Ask students what activities they do with their friends. List the responses on the board. Have students make either friendship flags or friendship flowers. Tell students they need to write "A friend is…." on their flower or flag and then write and/or illustrate qualities their friends should have.

Assessment
As students share their flag or flower, ask them to name a friend that has the quality they describe.

Activity 29 - More or Less

Grades: 1 - 3

Instructional Materials
- *Will I Have a Friend?* book, by Miriam Cohen
- craft materials to make friendship tokens
- copies of Attachment 31

Enduring Understanding
Making and keeping friends may help alleviate stress.

Guiding Question
Should you have a lot of friends or just a few friends?

Introduction
Show students some tokens of friendship such as necklaces, rings, bracelets, or Hawaiian leis. Ask students what they think these things have in common.

A. Read the story *Will I Have a Friend?*

B. Challenge students to identify the friendship token in the story.

C. Have students research one of the following friendship tokens: Hawaiian lei, Mexican amigo bracelet or the Native American friendship stick. Have them record facts about the significance of the token and how it is made.

D. Allow students to make a friendship token that conveys what they think friendship is about.

Assessment
Have students share the significance of their friendship token. Use the rubric on Attachment 31 to evaluate the tokens.

Attachment 31 — Friendship Token

Name _____ Score_____ /15

Content Standard	Standard	Student Assessment	Facilitator Assessment
I can clearly explain what my friendship token means to me.	3		
I have a well-made friendship token to share with the class.	3		
Skill Standard			
I had good eye contact with the audience.	3		
I had good volume during my presentation.	3		
My token is neat and large enough for the audience to see.	3		

4= Exceeds standard
3= Meets standard
2= Nearing standard
1= Below standard

Activity 30 - I Hate You

Grades: 1 - 5

Instructional Materials
The Hating Book by Charlotte Zolotow

Introduction
Ask students if they have ever had a friend that was very mad at them for no apparent reason. Discuss their situations. Ask each student if they ever found out the reason their friend was mad. Were they able to fix their friendship?

Enduring Understanding
Making and keeping friends may help alleviate stress.

Guiding Question
What do you do when you have a problem with a friend?

A. Read *The Hating Book*.

B. Ask students why they think the little girl was afraid to ask her friend why she was so mad. Discuss their responses. Explain that we make assumptions or inferences based on people's actions without ever finding out what the person was thinking.

C. Role play typical situations where people make assumptions.
- A friend walks by you. You say "Hi" and they don't respond. You assume. . .
- You left your favorite book on your desk. The only other person to enter the room was your friend. You come back in the room and your book is gone. You assume. . .
- There is indoor recess today. You go up to your friend to play, but they are already playing a game with other kids. You assume. . .

D. Invite students to determine what they could do in each situation instead of assuming the worst.

Assessment
Have students role-play their solutions to each situation to check for understanding.

Activity 31 - Priority Traits

Grades: 4 - 5

Instructional Materials
- adding machine tape
- sticky notes
- paper to make a book

Enduring Understanding
Making and keeping friends may help alleviate stress.

Guiding Questions
What qualities do you look for in a friend?
What qualities do you possess as a potential friend?

Introduction
Write the things you like about your best friend on the board. Ask students what they think the list is about. Tell students they are going to be making lists about friendship traits.

A. Give each student a strip of adding machine tape and some sticky notes. Ask students to list a quality of a good friend on each sticky note.

B. Have each student prioritize his or her list by placing the sticky notes in order of importance to the student.

C. Have students pair up and compare friendship quality lists. Have students change partners at least three times.

D. Discuss the traits in a friend the lists had in common. Why are these traits so important? Discuss why some traits were different. Do all of our friends exhibit all of these traits? Why do we have different friends with different qualities?

E. Have students make a friendship book by taking each sticky note and choosing a friend that is most like that trait. Have students list the trait and a picture of the friend. Continue with each trait to finish the friendship book.

Assessment
Have students share their friendship books and ask each student which friends are most like them and least like them. Ask them if it matters to them that their friends are different from each other.

UNIT 8

No one is perfect.

Activity 32 - Late Bloomers

Grades: K – 1

Instructional Materials

- *Leo the Late Bloomer* book, by Robert Kraus
- *Try and Stick With It* book, by Cheri J. Meiners
- paper plates
- construction paper
- black yarn
- markers
- copies of Attachment 25 from Activity 20

Enduring Understanding
No one is perfect.

Guiding Questions
What is perfectionism?
How do others influence your desire to be perfect?

Introduction

Write the word *perfectionism* on the board. Point out that it has the word perfect in it. Ask students what they think it means.

A. Read *Leo the Late Bloomer*.

B. Have students name all the things Leo could not do. List them on the board. Ask students how Leo's father feels about him. Ask them how Leo's mother feels. How do others influence your desire to be perfect (please others)?

C. Have students discuss how Leo's friends treated him throughout the story.

D. Invite students to make a Leo the Late Bloomer flower using Attachment 32.

E. Read *Try and Stick With It*.

F. Ask students to name three things they could not do, but now they can. Ask them how they were able to accomplish these new skills. Explain to students that if they were perfect, they would never learn new skills.

Assessment

Have students write a paragraph naming a skill they would like to learn and describing their plan to learn the skill.

Use the rubric on Attachment 20 to evaluate this activity.

88

Attachment 32   Late Blooming Flower Directions

1.   Cut out 5 flower petals using construction paper.

2.   On back of each petal, write something Leo could not do. Instead of writing, "Leo couldn't read," provide more details. For example, "Leo couldn't read his favorite Captain Underpants story."

3.   On the front of each petal, write something Leo was able to do by the end of the story. Be sure to give details in your sentence.

4.   Attach the petals to a paper plate using a stapler. Staple the petals with the back facing up, so when the petals are closed, you can read about what Leo could not do. When you open the petals by folding them out, you can read what Leo could do by the end of the story.

5.   Decorate the paper plate to look like Leo's face.

Activity 33 - Telling the Truth

Grades: 2 - 3

Instructional Materials
- *No, David* book, by David Shannon
- *David Gets in Trouble* book, by David Shannon
- *I Tell the Truth* book, by David Parker
- copies of Attachment 33

Enduring Understanding
No one is perfect.

Guiding Question
How can you be more honest?

Introduction
Have students discuss times they have been in trouble. Then ask students if they have lied so they would not get in trouble. Ask students if they know why they lied. Discuss the fact that we want to please others and ourselves, but we are not perfect. We all make mistakes. Relate a mistake you made that got you in trouble when you were a child. Describe what happened whether you lied or told the truth.

A. Read the stories *No, David* and *David Gets in Trouble*.

B. Go through the story *David Gets in Trouble* again. Ask students if David's troubles are accidents or poor choices by David. Ask students to decide in each case whether or not David is telling the truth. Discuss why David might tell a lie in that situation.
Read the book I Tell the Truth.

C. Invite students to revisit David's lies and role-play how he could tell the truth and make amends in each situation.

D. Discuss how telling the truth might get you in trouble, and you might have to make amends, but it will help you learn to make better decisions.

Assessment
Have students write a letter of apology to someone about a lie they told to stay out of trouble. Tell students they may choose whether they deliver the letters or not.

Use the rubric on Attachment 33 to evaluate the letters.

Attachment 33	Letter of Apology

Name _____ Score_____ /15

Content Standard	Standard	Student Assessment	Facilitator Assessment
I can clearly explain the lie I told to stay out of trouble.	3		
I have apologized and offered to make amends.	3		
Skill Standard			
Grammar and spelling are correct.	3		
Letter has an appropriate greeting, body and closing.	3		
Letter is neat and easy to read.	3		

4= Exceeds standard
3= Meets standard
2= Nearing standard
1= Below standard

Activity 34 - I Know I'm Supposed to Be Perfect

Grades: 4 - 5

Instructional Materials

- *Be a Perfect Person in Just Three Days!* book, by Stephen Manes
- green construction paper (or real broccoli)
- string
- copies of Attachment 27 from Activity 22

Enduring Understanding
No one is perfect.

Guiding Question
Should a person try to be perfect?

Introduction

Ask students if they ever feel pressured to be perfect because they are gifted. Discuss who puts the most pressure on them. Their parents? Their friends? Their teachers? Themselves?

A. Read chapters 1-3. Have students cut out a broccoli shape and wear it on a string like Milo. Have students go to a public area of the school like the library or the office to see how people react to the broccoli. Discuss with students how they felt while wearing the broccoli in the school.

B. Read chapter 4. Ask students if they ever had to skip a meal. How did they feel?

C. Read chapter 5. Have students try and sit without doing anything for five minutes. At the end of five minutes ask students to discuss how hard it is to do nothing.

D. Read chapter 6. Ask: How did Milo decide to deal with trying to be perfect? Was Milo happier when he was trying to be perfect or when he was just himself?

Assessment

Have each student write a speech and deliver it on the topic: Should a person try to be perfect? The speech should include one point for perfectionism, one point for not being perfect and the student's opinion on the topic.

Use the rubric on Attachment 22 to evaluate speeches.

Learning to Be a Durable Person

Grade Level and Materials Checklist

Activity	Grade Level	Materials Needed
1	K-5	brown paper bag tied with ribbon (1 per student) magazines note cards scissors zipper sandwich bags copies of Attachment 1
2	K-3	copies of Attachment 2
3	K-3	*I'm Gonna Like Me* book, by Jamie Lee Curtis drawing paper
4	3-5	sticky notes
5	K-5	paper (story boards and books) washable markers baby wipes copies of Attachment 3
6	K-5	copies of Attachments 4 and 5
7	1-5	foam peanuts toothpicks copies of Attachment 6 stickers and/or candy rewards (optional)
8	K-3	recycled materials basic arts and crafts supplies copies of Attachment 7
9	4-5	*Hooray for Diffendoofer Day* book, by Dr. Suess basic arts and crafts supplies recyclable material copies of Attachment 8
10	K-3	*I Am Responsible* book, by David Parker *I Show Respect* book, by David Parker *I'm in Charge of Me* book, by David Parker copies of Attachments 9 and 10
11	1-3	copies of Attachment 11 empty cereal boxes masking, packing or duct tape ribbon, flowers, feathers, pom pons, buttons, etc.
12	4-5	poster board markers or paint copies of Attachments 12 and 13
13	K-3	*I Accept You As You Are* book, by David Parker *It's Okay to be Different* book, by Todd Parr

		large drawing paper markers or crayons
14	4-5	*Don't Laugh At Me* book, by Steve Seskin and Allen Shamblin
15	K-5	copies of Attachments 14 and 15 drawing paper
16	K-3	*I Am Generous* book, by David Parker *Kids' Random Acts of Kindness* book, Foreword by Rosalynn Carter and Introduction by Dawna Markova large drawing paper markers or crayons copies of Attachments 16 and 17
17	4-5	1 large cut out heart per student copies of Attachment 18
18	K-5	Internet Multiple Intelligences Inventory 1 coat hanger per student small squares of paper 3" x 3" string or yarn copies of Attachment 20
19	K-3	hats for various careers copies of Attachments 21, 22, and 23
20	4-5	Internet access reference materials on various careers copies of Attachments 24 and 25 calculators
21	K-3	*Chrysanthemum* book, by Kevin Henke note cards drawing paper or recyclable material
22	4-5	copies of Attachment 26
23	3-4	*Stress Can Really Get On Your Nerves* book, by Trevor Romain & Elizabeth Verdick drawing paper
24	1-3	*Stress Can Really Get On Your Nerves* book, by Trevor Romain & Elizabeth Verdick copies of Attachments 28 and 29
25	K-5	*Today I Feel Silly* book, by Jamie Lee Curtis copies of Attachments 30 construction paper
26	K-5	*Alexander and the Terrible, Horrible, No Good, Very Bad Day* book, by Judith Viorst copies of the pamphlet, "What To Do When I'm Angry" from www.childrenshealthfund.org copies of Attachment 2 from Activity 2
27	K-1	*Do You Want to Be My Friend?* book, By Eric Carle *I'm a Good Friend* book, by David Parker

		washable finger paint large drawing paper
28	2-3	*Stevie* book, by John Steptoe construction paper markers or paint
29	1-3	*Will I Have a Friend?* book, by Miriam Cohen arts and crafts materials to make friendship tokens copies of Attachment 31
30	1-5	*The Hating Book* by Charlotte Zolotow
31	4-5	adding machine tape sticky notes paper to make a book
32	K-1	*Leo the Late Bloomer* book, by Robert Kraus *Try and Stick With It* book, by Cheri J. Meiners paper plates construction paper black yarn markers copies of Attachment 25 from Activity 20
33	2-3	*No, David* book, by David Shannon *David Gets in Trouble* book, by David Shannon *I Tell the Truth* book, by David Parker copies of Attachment 33
34	4-5	*Be a Perfect Person in Just Three Days!* book, by Stephen Manes green construction paper (or real broccoli) string copies of Attachment 27 from Activity 22

Note: Paper and pencils should be on hand each day, as should writing and illustration supplies, and may not be listed on the checklist.